THRONE *of* VICTORY

Michael and Julie Battaglini

ISBN 979-8-88943-577-8 (paperback)
ISBN 979-8-88943-578-5 (digital)

Christian Faith Publishing
832 Park Avenue
Meadville, PA 16335
www.christianfaithpublishing.com

Printed in the United States of America

PREFACE

These things I have spoken unto you that in me ye might have peace. In the world ye shall have tribulation but be of good cheer; I have overcome the world.

—John 16:33

Ever since I first read John 16:33, it has been a difficult verse for me. The reason for this is that it appears as though Jesus was telling His people that because He has had victory over something that is causing us pain (the world), then we should be encouraged, even though the thing which is causing us pain will continue to do so. For me, that didn't sound like much of a consolation. You see, no matter how much I may love, appreciate, or look up to someone who has overcome what I am still struggling with, and no matter how much I may be glad that they are no longer struggling with it, those feelings don't change the reality that the person who has overcome is still *someone other than me.* In other words, pain is still pain, toil is still toil, and tribulation is still tribulation, and I still have to walk through these things, experiencing them in all their painful glory, regardless of the Lord's victory over the world. *Or do I?*

The greatest treasure of the cross is found in what it has made us to be partakers of. Actually, this is a major understatement. The greatest treasure of the cross is really found in what it has made us to *be*. And John 16:33 carries such a depth to it when held up to the light of what has been done for us that once we begin to walk in the reality of what has been done we will never be the same.

These are not just words on paper. I have begun to experience it. I have begun to walk in the conscious awareness of His indwelling victory, and through this, I have learned that we are not merely partakers. His presence within us *transforms* us into people who can walk in the steady outworking of a new identity, the identity of the overcomer. And through this, we can become people who don't just walk *through* pain, toil, and tribulation but who walk *above* it.

Of course, stumbling and failure can still occur no matter where we are in our walk with Him, but the more we yield to His transformative process, the less they occur. And pain, toil, and tribulation do not disappear when we walk above them, but they become subservient and irrelevant when walking in the power of the Spirit. And these truths make what Jesus said in John 16:33 far more personal and far more powerful because He who has overcome now dwells within me and has transformed me on the deepest level into one who overcomes *with* Him. All that is left for me is to walk it out.

In pouring out His life at Calvary, Jesus joined everything He is in every way He could to every person who would receive Him. This means that your union with Him has transformed you, and He is no longer *someone other than you.* Of course, you are still two separate entities. He is God, and you are not, but now you are part of His body. This means we are no less bone of His bone and flesh of His flesh than an earthly wife is with her husband. This puts us into an entirely different place and experience with Him than many today are even aware of, though Scripture abounds with passages describing our relationship with Him in this light.

The letters contained in *Throne of Victory* are meant to draw your attention to one of the highest purposes of the anointing, which is your victory in the Lord, or rather, the *series* of victories He takes you through in this world as you walk in obedience. Each letter is set in order according to stages of growth and revelation, and each letter illuminates our advance through progressive levels of victory. Embedded throughout these pages are personal messages to you that He will bring out as you read. When you reach a word or a sentence or a series of sentences that speaks to you, pause there and meditate on what is being said. In this way, you will be enabled to apply what He is conveying to you and those elements of the overcomer that He has made you to be will be further brought out in your walk with Him.

The Lord has become one with His people in every possible way that He could. The same Spirit who raised Him from the dead, who facilitated His victory over the greatest of all enemies, now dwells in you and would have you know that the outworking of His victory in your life is His next mission. This book is meant to be used in tandem with the unction and guidance of His Spirit so that each stage of growth you go through may give way to a corresponding victory. If death has been conquered by the One who lives within you, then all things are truly yours, and every step you take by the Spirit who raised Christ from the dead is a component of some level of victory that He is leading you to. So apply these truths, as many as He will draw your attention to. It is His desire to empower you to grow from faith to faith and from victory to victory that you may point others to His heart and let them know that it is in His heart to see them become all that He has made them to be.

In Christ,
Michael Battaglini

Victory to you, my brothers and sisters in Christ,

Today's Scripture

> Purge me with hyssop and I shall be clean: wash me and I shall be whiter than snow. Make me to hear joy and gladness that the bones which thou hast broken may rejoice. Hide thy face from my sins and blot out all mine iniquities. (Psalm 51:7–9)

Today's Message: The Victory of Repentance

What do you first think of when you hear the word *repentance*? Have you ever felt the need to consider the path before you that you may embrace a higher one? Nothing less than honest soul-searching is needed to know where we are in relation to God. If we are distant, He calls us to Himself that we might find release from the pent-up pressures of sin and consequence and that He might open the floodgates of refreshing life to our souls. But we cannot truly give ourselves to Him unless we receive the convictions being pressed upon our hearts by His Spirit, but neither can we receive the truth that any hope exists beyond our struggles until we give ourselves to Him.

In our daily whirlwind of toil and striving, we often fail to understand God's timeframe. He has given space to each of us to consider our ways, to mend what is broken, and to build what is eternal. Undoubtedly we become dissatisfied with ourselves and our worldly failings. We want to accomplish something more, yet our days slip by, our minds are out of focus, and our hearts are burdened by our inevitable end. What we often miss is that God alone has all authority over life and death and that He is not bound by time as we are.

His understanding and power are infinite, and He is willing to do far more on our behalf than we dare believe, if only we would open our hearts to Him. Coming into contact with His ability to arrange and restore all things in perfect order will settle our fears. If we turn to Him and turn away from sin and darkness, we will come to trust in His power to carry us through. "My times are in thy hand…" (Psalm 31:15a). The human perspective is always shortsighted, but God has His eye on tomorrow with His hand on today.

Ever since man first turned from God, our basic drive has been to avoid anything that is perceived as a threat, including the revelation of our own weakness, wrongdoing, and failure. Pain, exposure to faults, and loss of stature have become mortal enemies. God is rich in mercy and willing to forgive but we cannot bear to face our own waywardness.

> For every one that doeth evil hateth the light, neither cometh to the light, lest his deeds should be reproved. (John 3:20)

We have been taught that our security is dependent upon what we accomplish. We must come to embrace the mystery that our value to God is all that matters and that it is only found in what Christ has accomplished. Those who believe that others hold the power to determine their significance will be reluctant to reveal anything that would cause man's estimation of them to diminish. Only when we turn to the Lord from our innermost being will we be freed from the pretense that holds us captive.

Repentance toward God is an explosion of life in the secret place of the heart. But how can we turn to Him if our heart is not softened? The motivation He takes hold of to draw us in is our yearning to see an end to our hopelessness and despair. The victory that brings us to our knees is a deep conviction of how far our sin has driven us from Him. Let us embrace this victory with wholehearted surrender to the Lord, "who will have all men to be saved and to come unto the knowledge of the truth" (1 Timothy 2:4).

Today's Prayer

Sovereign Lord, I am grateful that You have given Your all to bring me to this place. I offer myself fully to You this day that I may live and walk before You in truth. I humbly ask that You forgive me for all that I have done contrary to Your will, and I honor and glorify Your name above every name. Amen and amen.

Victory to you, my brothers and sisters in Christ,

Today's Scripture

> For they being ignorant of God's righteousness and going about to establish their own righteousness, have not submitted themselves unto the righteousness of God.
>
> For Christ is the end of the Law for righteousness to everyone that believeth. (Romans 10:3–4)

Today's Message: Paths of Righteousness

What does it mean to be justified before God? Is there significance in the work we accomplish and the sacrifices we make? Everything that the Lord has created and given to man is meant to be used in the building of His eternal Kingdom. Living a life that pleases Him means walking in obedience to the light that you have about His will for you. But right standing with God is a continual *experience* in which He reveals His heart and the mystery of what has been done to make you able to stand before Him. Does it move you to know that it is the revelation of who He is that causes you to draw near to Him and imparts the power to become His own? His mercy and grace abound to you, but His righteousness and perfection dwell within you if you are His.

Holiness is one of God's attributes, and only holiness can stand in His presence. Flesh and blood alone cannot attain this "for all have sinned and come short of the glory of God" (Romans 3:23). To be justified in His sight, we must relinquish the pride that causes us to set up our own standards of goodness and justice. It is the willingness of the heart and mind to receive the truth on these matters that pleases Him. By what is revealed in Scripture, we can know that right standing with God is possible but only through repentance, the cleansing of our sins by the atoning blood of Christ, and the indwelling of the Holy Spirit. What an amazing revelation that we can stand before God and not be seen with our sins but with the holiness and fulfillment of the Law that Christ has accomplished! We are made whole in His sight through our Lord Jesus Christ who took our sins upon Himself and caused us to appear before the Father clothed in His perfection.

Does it not seem that the true meaning of righteousness has become blurred? Right standing with God is a state of being, not a task to be accomplished.

> And if by grace, then is it no more of works: otherwise grace is no more grace. But if it be of works, then is it no more grace: otherwise work is no more work. (Romans 11:6)

The imputing of His righteousness to us and the revelation to our hearts that this work has been done produce an outflow of works, but we are not righteous *because* of our works. This act is a sacred gift, holy, and perfect. Our salvation produces a transformation within that changes our priorities, our conduct, and the paths we walk. God always begins in the heart, for it is there that He looks and there that He dwells.

We live in a fallen world full of vain philosophies and broken standards of goodness. We find ourselves grasping for something solid to hold onto without fully realizing the glory and importance of the work that has been done for us. We must learn where we are in relation to God and to the truth of Scripture. We are given only this short time to walk His paths and to sow the seeds of eternal inheritance. The more we abide in these truths, the less we can take with us of this world, but the freer and more victorious we will be.

Today's Prayer

Heavenly Father, I thank You for taking hold of my heart and drawing me into Yours. I thank You for allowing me to know You through the revelation of what You have done for me. It is not what I have done that brings me to You. It is through Christ alone and His victory at Calvary that I live in Your Spirit and walk this journey with You. In the mighty name of Jesus, amen.

Victory to you, my brothers and sisters in Christ,

Today's Scripture

> Let us draw near with a true heart in full assurance of faith, having our hearts sprinkled from an evil conscience and our bodies washed with pure water. (Hebrews 10:22)

Today's Message: Blessed Assurance

When your world stands still and the old familiar ache of uncertainty settles in where does your heart turn? What source of peace and safety do you reach for when the headwinds of life rush in and threaten to knock you down? The one solid assurance we can have, the one smooth path we can take on an otherwise rugged journey is our strong, abiding relationship with the Lord that will stand forever.

When we drift away from God, we become stagnant and blinded by the chaos and confusion around us. But we can draw near again with great liberty and boldness, regardless of our present struggles or past failures. We can come to Him with the utmost longing and yearning, knowing that He will always favor the seeking heart. The blessed assurance of who we are in Him and all He is in us will be imparted again to our souls like cool waters to parched lips as our cries for mercy ascend before His throne. His salvation, both temporal and eternal, rests upon His own grace and mercy and will uphold us to the end. Walking in this revelation requires purity of intent and a deep conviction that He alone has all power in Heaven and on Earth.

Everything purchased at the cross is poured freely upon us as we are open and able to receive it. The Lord has planted His very nature and all that He is into the core of our being, and He will accomplish far greater victories for us than the release from temporal struggles that we so earnestly seek. The rest that we desire to have in the midst of trials can only be based upon what we truly believe in and stand on. As our faith in His finished work grows, so grows our boldness because we no longer find our security in what *we* can do but in what *He* has done.

> In whom we have boldness and access with confidence by the faith of Him. (Ephesian 3:12)

The world is enduring mounting levels of social unrest, upheaval, and spiritual crisis that are being allowed by the Lord to awaken His people.

> In the fear of the Lord is strong confidence; and His children shall have a place of refuge. (Proverbs 14:26)

He desires to instill in us the conviction of our hope. He wants us to be deeply assured of His love and willingness to help and deliver. What we all have in common is the ability to recognize that He is the ultimate source of provision.

> And this is the confidence that we have in Him, that if we ask anything according to His will, He heareth us. (1 John 5:14)

His truth can fill our hearts as we make it our focus. As we obey and walk in steps ordained by His will, we will also walk in everything that pertains to His salvation in every realm, and we will stand under the unfailing power of His hand.

A divine atmosphere surrounds each of God's children. As it permeates our souls, we will demonstrate its effect in everything we do. We will reflect on the confidence that *He* has in *His own* power to walk us through it all. Once the reality of our strong connection to the One who cannot fail is settled within us, the process of growth and victory will flow naturally, revealing to others how holy, pure, and perfect He is in all His ways.

Today's Prayer

Abba Father, I thank You for the blessed assurance of Your unconditional love and perfect power and for the hope and peace I find in You and in everything You speak to me. I am deeply grateful that my relationship with You is continually growing and my heart is open to all that You are doing on my behalf because of Your great love for me. In Jesus's name, amen and amen.

Victory to you, my brothers and sisters in Christ,

Today's Scripture

> A new heart also will I give you and a new spirit will I put within you: and I will take away the stony heart out of your flesh and I will give you a heart of flesh. (Ezekiel 36:26)

Today's Message: Empower the Heart of Expectation

Do you believe that everything you are and everything you have comes from God alone? He dwells by His Spirit at the very center of your being. He has given you the most precious gift He could: Himself. The indwelling of His presence is a sacred miracle offered to all at great cost. Our expectancy in prayer, then, must be based upon the revelation of who He is and what He has already done for us. When our expectation arises, it activates our spiritual senses and allows us to commune with the Father in purity and transparency.

> Blessed are the pure in heart; for they shall see God. (Matthew 5:8)

Sometimes we pray and seek the Lord without truly believing that He will respond. All prayer according to His will must flow with the understanding that He will be faithful to answer. As our heart is moved by the revelation of His goodness, it awakens and empowers our confidence.

> My soul, wait thou only upon God; for my expectation is from Him. (Psalm 62:5)

When we allow anticipation to arise as we pray, we release ourselves from the burden of meeting the need ourselves because we are expressing that the power to bring forth the answer does not dwell within us. His solutions will manifest as the communication of our needs is grounded in the truth that He is even more willing to give than we are to receive. Surely He will accomplish things you never could have imagined and that are beyond your comprehension. He will never hinder what is best for you. Be stirred by the desire to glorify Him and to know His will for He will always be faithful to provide for you wherever He leads you. Receptivity to what He is saying about these matters balances us on every level.

> So shall the knowledge of wisdom be unto thy soul; when thou hast found it, then there shall be a reward and thy expectation shall not be cut off. (Proverbs 24:14)

When we have our thoughts established in His truth, the natural outflow will be that we commit our works and our concerns to Him. We must be committed to and dependent upon His grace for our expectation to flourish.

When you are challenged and struggling, are you willing to cleave to the Lord in faith? Sometimes we obsess over details when coping with life issues, but one thing we often forget to do is to search and find wise counsel from God.

> A wise man will hear and will increase learning; and a man of understanding shall attain unto wise counsels. (Proverbs 1:5)

When we are grateful and responsive to Him and abide in His truth, we speak strongly to His heart that He is everything to us. We may stumble when bearing burdens or navigating through tribulation, but our souls can still proclaim His goodness and mercy. In this, He is well pleased.

No human mind can fathom the power and wisdom employed by God as He transforms a heart by His grace. His children are intricately fashioned throughout a process involving His perfect understanding of all things. The Spirit of God purifies, preserves, and renews us. He teaches us that we are not sufficient to think or to speak anything wise or good of ourselves but that our sufficiency is of Him. In His great love, He bestows upon us every good and perfect gift as we rise to receive it that we may be conduits of His joy and kindness.

Today's Prayer

Papa God, I stand before Your holiness to glorify You at this moment and to give You thanks for all wisdom and understanding. Thank You for teaching me how to have a heart of expectation intertwined with Yours. As my time on Earth unfolds before You, I thank You that You provide such a wealth of spiritual blessings. I pray You would grant us all a deeper experiential knowledge of who You are to us in everything we do. In Jesus's name, amen and amen.

Victory to you, my brothers and sisters in Christ,

Today's Scripture

> Give ear, O ye heavens, and I will speak; and hear, O Earth, the words of my mouth. My doctrine shall drop as the rain, my speech shall distil as the dew, as the small rain upon the tender herb, and as the showers upon the grass. (Deuteronomy 32:1–2)

Today's Message: Eternal Wisdom

Have you ever admired the expression of wisdom? Heaven and Earth were created and established through the wisdom of God, and it is freely offered to His people regardless of our condition or status.

> If any of you lack wisdom, let him ask of God that giveth to all men liberally and upbraideth not and it shall be given him. (James 1:5)

The Lord is all wise and infinitely beyond wise. The beauty of His nature is that each of His attributes compliments the others. His wisdom reflects His vast goodness, infinite understanding, and absolute authority, and we will be provided with everything needed to walk confidently as we receive it at His hand.

By the Spirit of God within and by the written Word of God illuminated by the Spirit, we will know what to do and how to do it. Yet many don't seek Him when pressured by time or gripped with adversity. We often try to fix problems ourselves, getting ahead of Him and acting without His counsel. Stepping back, becoming still, and letting His hand move allow Him to work out things that are burdening us and give us space to perceive what He is saying. It cannot be by our understanding but by His provision and guidance that we have victory. He knows what everyone around us is thinking even before their thoughts are formed and their actions planned. His wisdom cannot exist without His perfect knowledge. This is why He is the only one we should rely on when facing troubling situations or struggles with people. Each difficulty has its own God-given solution that stands before you waiting to be received and implemented. Simply turn to Him and be open as He infuses understanding into your heart and mind.

> Hear counsel and receive instruction that thou mayest be wise in thy latter end. (Proverbs 19:20)

The very essence of the wisdom of God begins to take hold within us when our heart is intertwined with His and our spiritual eyes are opened to His Word. It is in this place that we receive His anointing to walk in all ways as we are called. All insight, discernment, discretion, and vision follow to carry out His will in all things, imparting to others that which has been poured into us.

> Let the word of Christ dwell in you richly in all wisdom; teaching and admonishing one another in psalms and hymns and spiritual songs, singing with grace in your hearts to the Lord. (Colossians 3:16)

Sometimes we don't understand what the Lord is doing. He uses the most unusual circumstances, even sickness, sorrow, and man's sin to achieve His purposes. It all revolves around His eternal plan and your eternal inheritance. It seems He is creating a magnificent mystery, reassuring and sustaining us through it all to trust Him more and to draw closer to our first love. Do you wonder sometimes why He is putting you to the test in a seemingly private and personal way, a way that no one around you is aware of? It is so you would look to Him alone. Surely we all need to learn the importance of total trust in Him. When life doesn't make sense, look to the author and finisher of your faith. He knows everything about everything. He even knows everything that *could* happen. His wisdom, freely given and received, brings His plans for you to their fulfillment and to their perfect end. Through your trust and obedience, all things will fall into place in His perfect time.

Today's Prayer

Gracious Father, I thank You that You open my heart to know the truth, and that You open my ears to hear what You are saying. Your direction and sound guidance is all I need to do the right thing and to have the proper perspectives that You may be glorified with each step that I take. In Jesus's name, amen and amen.

Victory to you, my brothers and sisters in Christ,

Today's Scripture

> And the Spirit of the Lord shall rest upon Him, the spirit of wisdom and understanding, the spirit of counsel and might, the spirit of knowledge and of the fear of the Lord; And shall make Him of quick understanding in the fear of the Lord and He shall not judge after the sight of His eyes, neither reprove after the hearing of His ears. (Isaiah 11:2–3)

Today's Message: Wise in the Spirit

Is it possible to abide in a manifestation of wisdom that arises solely by the Spirit of God? Is it something you already have available to you but have not yet walked in? The way most people navigate through life is to absorb information, process it, and act on it. Some seem to have a natural ability to quickly take in their surroundings and stay one step ahead of others. But those who belong to the Lord are called to operate beyond what we perceive with our physical senses. We are called to grow to a place where we can offer and apply wise counsel that transcends earthly reasoning. This type of insight does not come from experience or natural perception. It comes from the Spirit of God and is drawn out through prayer.

It can be difficult for our minds to recognize the sovereignty of the Lord over everything that is taking place in the world. In these perilous times, we sometimes struggle to keep our head above the sea of distractions and deceptions swirling around us. The constant pulsing of images and voices projected by entertainment and media threatens to numb our senses and pull us from our calling. Even among the people of God, we are met with a continual stream of voices claiming to speak for Him.

> Beloved, believe not every spirit, but try the spirits, whether they are of God: because many false prophets are gone out into the world. (1 John 4:1)

We can learn to recognize the voice of wisdom within us because of its perfect clarity, soundness, and precision. At its foundation is a heart that seeks after God in prayer, longing for His counsel and guidance in all things. Applying the wisdom of the Spirit in the way that He leads will make the much-needed difference in a world that is crying out for answers and direction. This grace upon His child is more effectual than all the worldly knowledge available to mankind.

Sometimes we are unable to discern what the Lord is saying because we're filled with the thinking and perceptions of the natural realm. The more we learn to draw from the Spirit, the easier it will be for us to determine what is right, good, and God's will and to demonstrate in love and power the genuineness of His touch. Undoubtedly, many are filled with earthly methods of reasoning and seem to excel as a result, but the wisdom of God is different. It is different in the way it is applied and in the fruit of the lives that become peaceable and powerful as a result.

> But the wisdom that is from above is first pure, then peaceable, gentle, and easy to be intreated, full of mercy and good fruits, without partiality and without hypocrisy. (James 3:17)

When we learn to detect and follow the messages that are gently pressed upon our hearts and minds by the Spirit, our understanding of what will occur when we follow His lead will be enhanced. Our sensitivity to Him and our judgment about proper courses of action will be refined. If you've never done it, allow yourself to begin asking for direction in the decisions that you make throughout your day. The fruit of this practice will be seen in the circumstances and people around you that change as a result, but it will also produce a powerful and lasting effect upon you.

Today's Prayer

Blessed are You, Lord, who brings forth wisdom and guidance by Your Spirit. Thank You for granting me the ability to walk with You in a manner that glorifies You, to follow the narrow path that You have set before me, and to live a life that is truly Spirit-led and Spirit-filled. In Jesus's name, amen and amen.

Victory to you, my brothers and sisters in Christ,

Today's Scripture

> And I will restore to you the years that the locust hath eaten, the cankerworm and the caterpillar and the palmerworm, my great army which I sent among you. And ye shall eat in plenty and be satisfied and praise the name of the Lord your God that hath dealt wondrously with you: and my people shall never be ashamed. And ye shall know that I am in the midst of Israel and that I am the Lord your God and none else: and my people shall never be ashamed. (Joel 2:25–27)

Today's Message: Unstoppable Restoration

In your walk with the Lord, have you ever found yourself in need of restoration? Wherever the people of God go, new life follows. Though we may stray from the wisdom and guidance of the Spirit, He is faithful to restore us from our failures and, at times, even from our successes. We live in a culture immersed in distractions that can open us up to attack if we allow ourselves to be drawn away by them. If we stumble, His power and provision are there to restore us, for He is unwavering in His devotion to us.

> He restoreth my soul: He leadeth me in the paths of righteousness for His name's sake. (Psalm 23:3)

Oftentimes, misery and desperation awaken us when we are going in the wrong direction, and we suddenly realize that we have been unrealistic about our ability to choose our own path. As we humbly repent before the Lord, we can embrace the assurance that we will be brought back into our place and that what has been broken or taken away will be restored.

The assurance of restoration is a mystery of God's glory. Throughout our walk, He brings healing and deliverance, but His work goes much deeper, to the very core of our crisis.

> And she shall bring forth a Son and thou shalt call His name Jesus, for He shall save His people from their sins. (Matthew 1:21)

We are made free, not only from the consequences of our sin but from the very sin itself that drives us from Him. Those who give themselves to this work will experience total victory.

When we have come to a place of rest and healing in the Lord, when we have been restored again to His inner leading, we are exhorted to bring to remembrance everything He has done for us.

> I will remember the works of the Lord: surely I will remember thy wonders of old. I will meditate also of all thy work and talk of thy doings. (Psalm 77:11–12)

As we commit ourselves to Him in the midst of our liberty as much as we did in the midst of our need, we will be equipped with everything necessary to continue walking His path.

The promise of the Lord to restore stands no matter what. In our failures, in our struggles, and in our storms, we are offered hope when all else has failed.

> "For I will restore health unto thee and I will heal thee of thy wounds," saith the Lord; "because they called thee an outcast saying, 'This

> is Zion, whom no man seeketh after.'" (Jeremiah 30:17)

Scripture is filled with testimonies of healing and renewal, of total power and love that flow from the Saviour, and of revelations that strengthen our trust in Him. He is the master restorer of humanity. His ways transcend medicine, human values, and all the attempts of society to save itself. The work that is manifested for us reinforces the biblical truth that restoration can come only from God. Our approach must be to connect our hearts and minds with perspectives that are based on the truth of His nature. When we do this, it will change us. The Lord is on an unstoppable quest to rescue and revive His people and as long as we are willing and cooperate with His work, nothing will deter Him.

Today's Prayer

Abba Father, I humbly bless Your name today. Thank You for Your faithfulness to reestablish me in every way as I yield to You. Thank You for restoring me to truth and obedience to what You have called me to at this hour. In the mighty name of Jesus, amen and amen.

Victory to you, my brothers and sisters in Christ,

Today's Scripture

> For therein is the righteousness of God revealed from faith to faith: as it is written, the just shall live by faith. (Romans 1:17)

Today's Message: Immovable Faith

Have you ever considered the process by which you are equipped to walk in faith? What is this assurance of hope we carry that causes us to bear witness to the eternal, even as we struggle in the temporal? Our works in the Lord, even the works we exhibit in our weakness, testify that the revelation we hold is genuine, for our awareness of Him is not based on feelings or emotions. It doesn't fluctuate with success or failure. It is a conviction and an understanding that leads to an expression, however imperfect. To walk with God is to carry an inward knowledge that has come by revelation, signifying that we are a people who have come to rest upon an immovable foundation.

We all desire to understand what is happening around us, to grasp the meaning of events that beset us and cause us pain. But the truth is that none would be able to stand or walk or live in the absence of the work being done *for* us. The Lord is constantly altering the unseen to serve our greater good, to bring us into the inheritance chosen for us from eternity, and to establish our place in His house.

> Surely goodness and mercy shall follow me all the days of my life and I will dwell in the house of the Lord forever. (Psalm 23:6)

His faithfulness is the sure foundation upon which we rest, whether we are truly resting in it or not. We are kept by the One whom we believe in, whether we are expressing this belief properly or not. Faith manifests in many ways, but at its core, it is unreserved confidence in the God who has proven Himself. His love, His power, and His willingness to help are richly demonstrated and given abundant witness before us, regardless of our responses. This revelation alone, this unveiling of His way with us, will imprint upon our hearts the testimony of His unfailing love.

Sometimes when we are on the brink of realizing some great milestone or breakthrough, we find instead breakdowns, trials, and stretching. It is important to relinquish our grip on how we think things should be and at what time. We will surely find release from this assault on our faith, as we have from all others, and we will stand in the victory that our Father has ordained. We cannot come into a faith that is immovable through mentally grasping at things that can only be grasped by the heart. This is the purpose of refinement. Our trials make way for the fervent seeking and enlargement of the heart that are necessary to hold the greater faith, the greater victory, and the greater reward.

> For he that cometh to God must believe that He is and that He is a rewarder of them that diligently seek Him. (Hebrews 11:6b)

The Lord will frequently intervene in the affairs of those who trust in His power to save, forgive, and restore. In this season, we are all facing unpredictable conditions, and the troubles of fallen humanity are increasing. Portions of the tribulation and struggle around us will be allowed into our lives at times to purify our walk with Him, but He will always make a way for us to endure and overcome. Don't be discouraged or frustrated when things take a different course than the one you expected. Instead, refocus and keep going because He never stops redeeming and restoring. He is continually working with you to see whether you understand just how intimately He is providing for your every need throughout each leg of your journey.

Today's Prayer

Abba Father, I thank You for strengthening my faith in times of uncertainty and for grounding my trust in You. You have never ceased to provide for me, to pour out Your mercy, and to sustain me in all that I do that I might bear fruit in obedience. Thank You, Father, for Your steadfast love for me. In Jesus's name, amen and amen.

Victory to you, my brothers and sisters in Christ,

Today's Scripture

> But God, who is rich in mercy, for His great love wherewith He loved us, even when we were dead in sins, hath quickened us together with Christ (by grace ye are saved). (Ephesians 2:4–5)

Today's Message: Irrevocable Mercy

When you consider everything that the Lord has done for you, what resonates the most in your heart? In what ways has His kindness moved you to more fully center yourself on Him? A profound emptiness dwells at the center of humanity. Society glorifies high status and gives itself to frenzied busyness to achieve it, all in a vain attempt to ignore the gaping void within. As a result, we are all perpetual victims of a whirlwind of activity pressing in upon us with self-serving agendas and demands. Many of us end up completely unable to express gratitude or to appreciate the good gifts from the Lord that fall daily into our laps. Yet there exists a place unknown to carnal experience that is not polluted by these influences and where we can focus upward, free from the howling storms of struggle, strife, and self. It is a place of revelatory victory where we can pour out even as the Lord has poured into us. It is here where we are no longer driven away from showing compassion to the hurting and where we no longer quench the stirrings in our heart that rouse us to minister to the Saviour and His people.

> And the Lord passed by before him and proclaimed, "The Lord, the Lord God, merci-

> ful and gracious, longsuffering, and abundant in goodness and truth." (Exodus 34:6)

Appreciating the mercy of God can be difficult because our fallen nature, sensing its own faults, seeks to project justice and the need for forgiveness onto others. We look at those who have entangled themselves in cycles of sin and failure, and our natural inclination is to allow them their struggles and to stand aloof from their just recompense. But the mercy of God extends to the greatest offenses and to the worst offenders. He doesn't seek to issue the punishment deserved and doesn't wish to leave any of us drowning in our sin. He asks that we accept the work He has done and that He is willing to do on our behalf and that we would seek the same for others.

> Who is a God like unto thee that pardoneth iniquity and passeth by the transgression of the remnant of His heritage? He retaineth not His anger forever, because He delighteth in mercy. (Micah 7:18)

The mercy of God toward humanity is irrevocable. We are only separated from it by our refusal to receive it. He offers pardon though He knows the depth of our guilt. He offers healing and deliverance, whether our sickness and bondage arise from our sin or not. All-encompassing and unrelenting is His will to release us from our afflictions of flesh and soul. We will be brought to humility at the revelation of His great and tender mercy. With power yet to be revealed against His enemies, He withholds a just condemnation from all who receive Him. Jesus died that mercy could be extended in every way, to every degree, and to every person.

Each morning, God's children awake into a renewing atmosphere surrounding their soul and to the beauty of His voice speaking in their spirit. If we get up on the wrong side of the bed, we will find His love waiting for us there as well. We will surely have our ups and downs, and we will grow weary, but through it all, fresh currents of grace and mercy flow down to us. He does not love as man loves but pours out kindness from an endless supply and an eternal existence.

Today's Prayer

As I behold my Father in Heaven, who has graciously granted me eternal mercy to stand in, I pray You would uphold me in all that comes my way. Thank You, Father, that Your mercy revitalizes my spirit each moment that I may praise and exalt You, my most high God. In Jesus's name, amen and amen.

Victory to you, my brothers and sisters in Christ,

Today's Scripture

> Looking unto Jesus, the author and finisher of our faith; who for the joy that was set before Him endured the cross, despising the shame, and is set down at the right hand of the throne of God. (Hebrews 12:2)

Today's Message: Unspeakable Joy

Have you experienced the freedom to rejoice in everything that the Lord is to you and all that you are to Him? Joy is Heaven's gift to the redeemed, but it is sometimes foreign to us until we go deeper in our walk. Many of God's people have endured great suffering, yet they possess the capacity to delight in His will and remain in that place regardless of what they are facing. The Saviour's joy comes from His desire to please the Father and to abide in Him. It is both the cause and the effect of His obedience and unbroken communion with Him. He wants this reality to be ours that our hearts would be full and our strength certain.

Lasting joy cannot be found in the rapidly fluctuating conditions around us, nor can it be based on our fickle emotions but on the revelation of the deep and abiding love of the Father for us. It is dependent upon who He is, how He feels about us, and what He does in relation to us and why. This is a deep, transcendent, and timeless reality that we can behold with our hearts in any season, whether things are going well with us or not. Once we begin to experience His favor in the midst of our trials, we will be far more willing to set our affection on things above.

We will indeed find rest in the everlasting covenant. In the end, we will freely and joyfully give everything we are back to the Lord for His glory. The systems and institutions of this world can collapse in a moment under the weight of man's sin, but the desire of the Father is to restore His children and to allow us to experience His faithfulness and mercy that the fullness of His joy may be ours. His enduring delight in us is a place of refuge for our souls. It stands as a bulwark against our ever-shifting circumstances. It will strengthen us to prevail until the end, for when Jesus took our sins upon Himself, we were restored to a peace with God that cannot be broken and to a joy that will stand forever.

Our willingness to rejoice doesn't always materialize in the way we would expect it to. Struggles and brokenness can come suddenly, but the Lord is always there to rescue us and restore our souls. As a result, we choose to seek and search out His wisdom in exchange for our own. The self-discipline, obedience, and accountability of a life guided and guarded by the Holy Spirit produce a foundational joy that builds steadily within us. His ways are simple, direct, and full of hope, but they are sometimes, especially at the start, beyond our ability to perceive.

The joy of the Lord springs from the very essence of His glory. True restoration of your heart can only come from what He communicates to you about the depth of His love for you. His joy radiates throughout Creation and through the gifts He bestows upon His people. It shifts our hearts to a place of worship because it doesn't change or fade, nor is it something we can create, earn, or deserve. Though we had nothing to offer Him, He came to us and died for us that we may live and experience His love forever.

> And the ransomed of the Lord shall return and come to Zion with songs and everlasting joy upon their heads. They shall obtain joy and gladness, and sorrow and sighing shall flee away. (Isaiah 35:10)

Today's Prayer

Papa God, I thank You for letting me experience Your joy that gives hope and peace to my soul. Thank You for shifting darkness into light and suffering into gladness that I may walk with Your perspectives instead of my own and that I may keep my heart forever fixed on You. In Jesus's name, amen and amen.

Victory to you, my brothers and sisters in Christ,

Today's Scripture

> In the beginning God created the heaven and the earth. And the earth was without form and void; and darkness was upon the face of the deep. And the Spirit of God moved upon the face of the waters. (Genesis 1:1–2)

Today's Message: Timeless Creation

Have you ever considered the truth that everything in Creation was formed as an expression of the heart of God, who has no beginning and no end? The meaning behind what He has made is vast, and no one can fathom its extent or magnitude. Our eyes have seen it, and our ears have heard it, yet much of it is taken for granted because we are told that it does not reflect eternal truth or the eternal attributes of God. The human mind can hardly conceive of what came before and what will come after, yet it rationalizes, debates, and ignores the significance of Creation.

> He hath made everything beautiful in His time; also He hath set the world in their heart, so that no man can find out the work that God maketh from the beginning to the end. (Ecclesiastes 3:11)

Time may not be visible but its effects are. Our points of reference are the benchmarks of change that indicate its passage. But time and change were not factors in the beginning. They were set in place outside of God's existence, for He is eternal and does not change. For Him, there is no time, nor space, nor boundary, nor limit. We are grateful indeed to be given this earthly beginning to our eternal destiny that we may gain the knowledge, experience, and wisdom necessary to serve as the foundation of our Kingdom inheritance. And as the Spirit of God moved upon the waters at Creation, He moves again upon His people to bring forth heirs fit to inherit this new Heaven and Earth.

Creation reveals the touch of God's glory to each of us. It proclaims His living Word. It engulfs our senses and declares the attributes of His divinity, even as He dwells in realms beyond the perception of our physical senses. No one can say that He is silent toward them. In beholding what He has made, we may only grasp the revelation of His Person in part, but in so doing, we perceive Him as He is: without beginning or end, infinite, and omnipotent.

> The Lord reigneth, He is clothed with majesty; the Lord is clothed with strength wherewith He hath girded Himself: the world also is established that it cannot be moved. Thy throne is established of old: thou art from everlasting. (Psalm 93:1–2)

It is well within our reach to receive what He is speaking. His eternal power and divine nature are spoken of in everything He has made. So let it be known that "all things were made by Him and without Him was not anything made that was made" (John 1:3). His majesty and magnificence are represented by the beauty and greatness of everything that is.

May the truths and decrees of all created order consume the deepest part of your heart as they manifest the Word of God to you and speak revelation and truth. Just as nothing in Creation was made in vain, nothing in your small world will ever be wasted by the Lord. Every detail is known and brought together for your good. Most importantly, all that He has created, including you, bears the mark of victory because it reveals His glory, power, wisdom, and majesty.

It is all designed that we may know the One whom we serve, that we may learn who we are in Him, and that we may find our place in His house. The deeper we go in His Spirit, the more our own understanding will give way to revelatory glimpses of the meaning behind it all. Everything has been lovingly and perfectly prepared by Him that we may behold the greatness of His heart.

Today's Prayer

Blessed are You, Lord, our Majesty, who brings forth the beautiful grandeur of Creation to enhance each moment of our lives with You. Thank You for the deep and fulfilling moments that You give us to ponder, reflect, and meditate on the significance of everything You have made. In Jesus's name, amen and amen.

Victory to you, my brothers and sisters in Christ,

Today's Scripture

> Then said He, "Lo, I come to do thy will, O God". He taketh away the first that He may establish the second. By the which will we are sanctified through the offering of the body of Jesus Christ once for all. (Hebrews 10:9–10)

Today's Message: Sanctified in His Holiness

What comes to mind when you think of the holiness of God? His very existence radiates wonders, seen and unseen, and everything He touches is made pure. Have you ever considered that His very presence within you sanctifies you? His essence is distinct and separate from ours but as believers in Messiah, as members of His body, we are set apart to continue the expansion of His everlasting Kingdom. And we have been chosen to do it in the same power and favor bestowed upon Him by the Father. This is what it means to be sanctified. Each of us is called to minister and to mentor in the capacity and time of His choosing because we are the place of His habitation and the extension of His grace.

> For ye are the temple of the living God; as God hath said, "I will dwell in them and walk in them; and I will be their God and they shall be my people. Wherefore come out from among them and be ye separate," saith the Lord, "and touch not the unclean thing; and I will receive you. And will be a Father unto you, and ye

> shall be my sons and daughters," saith the Lord Almighty. (2 Corinthians 6:17–18)

The natural man contradicts and misjudges holiness, but as the age of fallen men passes, the blindness and corruption of the age pass with it. The world has been subjected to multilayered deceptions and wicked spiritual influences, but as God's children, we are separated unto Him. Because of our rebirth in His Spirit, our very essence and identity are now sanctified unto Him. This is why all attempts by our flesh to live contrary to this new reality leave us feeling deeply unsatisfied and disjointed.

The holiness of the Lord is distinct, pure, supremely excellent, and entirely perfect. Its essence and manifestation are that of absolute separation from sin. When man fell, everything in Creation was affected by sin. Even our ability to grasp the depth of love and purity in the heart of God has been deeply altered by the fall. As we stand before Him, sanctified by His presence, His righteous judgments are revealed, and His verdicts rendered. We are no longer separated from Him, for when He sees us, He sees His own righteousness, and our sins are washed away. The world has been polluted, devoured, and destroyed by the covetousness of fallen humanity. The Lord sees it all. Everything upon the earth is known and recorded, but the sin of those who are bought by the blood of Christ will be forgotten forever. This is the heritage of those redeemed by His sacrifice.

> And such were some of you: but ye are washed, but ye are sanctified, but ye are justified in the name of the Lord Jesus and by the Spirit of our God. (1 Corinthians 6:11)

Scripture places great emphasis on the fact that we are to walk out a sanctified life, but the process by which we achieve this can only begin as we recognize what has been done for us and what we now are. It is not our personal holiness that sets us apart. We are clothed in the glory and righteousness of Jesus Christ, and everything flows out from that grace. The work of redemption encompasses every aspect of human need, including and especially our need to stand before the holiness of God as those who are as separate from sin as He is. This is the power of the cross.

Today's Prayer

My Father in Heaven, as your grace resonates within my soul, I know my life is in Your hands for guidance and provision, for me to grow and learn, acknowledging my weaknesses and strengths. Take all that I am, and lead me forward as I grow to become more and more like You. In Jesus's name, amen and amen.

Victory to you, my brothers and sisters in Christ,

Today's Scripture

> Abide in me and I in you. As the branch cannot bear fruit of itself, except it abide in the vine; no more can ye, except ye abide in me. I am the vine, ye are the branches: He that abideth in me and I in him, the same bringeth forth much fruit: for without me ye can do nothing. (John 15:4–5)

Today's Message: The Harvest of Obedience

Is a hunger to do the will of God the defining characteristic of your life? It has been ordained by the Lord that each of His children would fulfill a part of His eternal design, regardless of our shortfalls and imperfections. The call to yield to His will is a call to you, for you have been chosen to birth into this realm a unique manifestation of His Kingdom. You are in place according to His wisdom, created to bring forth from this generation a portion of His eternal inheritance in the saints. Obedience to this means a total abandonment of the heart to the love of God and to everything that His love asks of you.

For each of us, the call to salvation is a call to receive Jesus as Lord and to find our place in His house and at His table. Jesus is the ultimate demonstration of obedience. By the empowerment of His Spirit, we too can walk in the manifestation of His total submission to the will of the Father.

> Jesus saith unto them, "My meat is to do the will of Him that sent me and to finish His work." (John 4:34)

Joyful are those who obey Him and search for His direction in all that they do and with all their hearts. Don't settle for anything less. Acquire from Him the plan and the process that will lead you to grow to your full stature.

The Lord has sown into you His very Spirit and Person. Allow Him to reap a harvest of obedience that will lead you to such richness and fulfillment that you will rise up and proclaim the glory of this life to others. It will spread among His people, inspiring, empowering, and edifying all who come to embrace it. It will lead to a bountiful ingathering of spiritual fruit by a people identified by their zeal to give of themselves and to serve in His house. We will all excel in our maturity, abiding in the life of the vine and leading others to eternal paths.

Sometimes our resolve to obey the Spirit's leading is eroded by the pressures and distractions around us. Cultivating a life of obedience means working with Him in the sanctification of our priorities, affections, and associations. We are all called to expand the mission field in the way and time of His choosing. We all have but one life, one chance, and one purpose to labor for in the greatest and most important work of our time.

> Then saith He unto his disciples, "the harvest truly is plenteous but the laborers are few; Pray ye therefore the Lord of the harvest, that He will send forth laborers into his harvest." (Matthew 9:37:38)

As we grow in these truths, the avenues we are led down will bring us to our place in the glorious conclusion of this age. Our heart will overflow with gratitude for the priceless opportunity we have been given. True obedience in the Kingdom is an experience of spiritual life that comes as a result of our yielding to the perfect obedience of Christ within us. The best part of abiding in Him *is* abiding in Him. Let us enjoy the unbroken communion of His Spirit and fill Heaven with the souls and fruit that will follow.

Today's Prayer

Dear heavenly Father, I thank You for helping me to walk in obedience as part of my worship of You. Please cleanse me of everything that hinders my body, soul, and spirit from being a living sacrifice unto You. Let submission to Your will take precedence in me to serve and to live my life to the fullest at Your command. My heart is Yours alone. In Jesus's name, amen and amen.

Victory to you, my brothers and sisters in Christ,

Today's Scripture

> The Spirit of the Lord is upon me, because He hath anointed me to preach the Gospel to the poor; He hath sent me to heal the brokenhearted, to preach deliverance to the captives and recovering of sight to the blind, to set at liberty them that are bruised, to preach the acceptable year of the Lord. (Luke 4:18–19)

Today's Message: The Power of the Overflow

Have you recognized the need to draw deep from the well of life within you that you may continue the path you are called to? The fountain of God in the heart of every believer brings forth the power to revive and restore. He will prepare you for the challenges ahead. He will create a way through the times we live in and the times that are coming, through the midst of affliction, trouble, and confusion. He has carried you often when you felt like giving up. You may rest in great confidence, knowing and remembering that you abide with a faithful companion.

> There is a friend that sticketh closer than a brother. (Proverbs 18:24b)

When your countenance falls, the light of His glory will shine upon you and change tears of sorrow into tears of joy. Such encounters with Him bring the highest joy because they bridge the deepest divide between hurt and healing. You will be anointed with a living hope that will overflow to touch those appointed to hope.

Do you yearn for a greater infilling of the Spirit than you are now experiencing? Sometimes we plan, arrange, and communicate what arises from our own mind and will but letting Him flow freely means releasing our agendas. As we walk with Him in simple openness to His will and cultivate a heart of expectation, we will see our hope manifesting in all realms. We tend to complicate things as we seek to walk out His will, but His way is always simple. As we seek Him with our whole heart, His anointing and power will overflow in ways we could never have imagined.

The glory of the Lord is perfect light and power to our spirit, soul, and body. As our eye is single and focused on His leading, our whole being follows and is full of light. The world is full of distractions and dismay, but light and darkness cannot occupy the same space at the same time. Arrest the voices of darkness that clamor for your attention and focus on the Light that has so often lifted you into who you really are.

> Casting down imaginations and every high thing that exalteth itself against the knowledge of God and bringing into captivity every thought to the obedience of Christ. (2 Corinthians 10:5)

Do you long for the Lord to flow freely through you? Are you ready to serve, stand, and yield that a unique manifestation of His light would shine through you? Though He was battered and broken at the cross, He was resurrected by the same Spirit who filled the upper room at Pentecost and who dwells in us today in presence and power.

> But we all, with open face beholding as in a glass the glory of the Lord, are changed into the same image from glory to glory, even as by the Spirit of the Lord. (2 Corinthians 3:18)

Without Him, we can't function as the people we are called to be. He reminds us to stay conscious of our connection to Him and yielded to His guidance that we may overflow with everything He is to us. Each time He ministers through us, we will be touched by the very power flowing out of us and will be changed as a result. We will find ourselves becoming the expressions of His inexpressible nature. Let Him consume you with the outflow of His grace. Receive and know that He is about to do a greater work in you than you have yet seen.

Today's Prayer

Abba Father, I thank You for filling me with the fire of Your Holy Spirit. As I walk this journey, I rejoice with each step, knowing that You are with me. I have great confidence that no matter what is ahead, You will speak and extend grace and mercy to me. I bless You, Lord, my great Comforter. In Jesus's name, amen.

Victory to you, my brothers and sisters in Christ,

Today's Scripture

> And Peter answered Him and said, "Lord, if it be thou, bid me come unto thee on the water". And He said, "Come". And when Peter was come down out of the ship, he walked on the water, to go to Jesus. (Matthew 14:28–29)

Today's Message: Walk on the Water

Do you believe it is possible to live above the power and influence of this fallen world? The Lord's offer to Peter to come to Him on the water carries a personal invitation to each of us to learn how to walk above the effects of the world by the power of His Spirit. Everything Jesus did and does is instructive in nature. He teaches through His actions and each lesson carries multiple layers of truth. He is the Word of God made flesh and to behold His works is to hear Him speak.

Each time we take a step by the leading of the Spirit, whether in ministry to others or in our everyday activities, we are brought to a higher plane of existence and experience. Each act of obedience brings us deeper into the Spirit and enhances a relationship that transcends the dominion of flesh and blood. Our faith in His name and willingness to be led will bring us to a level of connection with Him which by its very nature causes the laws and forces of the natural realm to yield. Why then do we wish to see our days as divided between the work of Heaven and the work of Earth, between the sanctified and the ordinary? Anywhere He takes us can be consecrated to serve our role in His house. Indeed, this is His desire and delight, so let us seek Him for the glorious removal of any such distinction. We are called to a place of steady revelatory reflection where our growth is enhanced and our awareness heightened no matter where we find ourselves.

> But we all, with open face beholding as in a glass the glory of the Lord, are changed into the same image from glory to glory, even as by the Spirit of the Lord. (2 Corinthians 3:18)

Before we are equipped to stand against the wind and waves, we must learn to walk in the Spirit, to walk on the water. But our first step out of the boat, out of the security we find in the things of the natural realm, requires recognition of *where* the Lord is. Is He calling you to the water? Is He asking you to remove yourself from the security mechanisms you have trusted in your whole life that He may bring you into a deeper experience? We are safe, not in the present means by which He has made us safe but in Him alone and in the place He is calling us.

If it be thou, bid me to come unto thee on the water… As we begin to perceive where the Lord is and where He is leading us, hunger and passion will rise up within us to *be* where He is. It is not our personal courage that empowers us to step out of the boat but a strong desire to be where we are called and a deep abiding trust that He will only take us where provision is made. Are you willing to forsake your dreams of a safe and secure life in the confines of natural experience, knowing that He will not fail to secure a much better place for you? Sometimes we are moved to action by our unmanageable conditions. The battle presses hard upon us, and we become dissatisfied with the toys and trinkets that have always distracted us from our deeper longings. It is then that we see Him on the water, and our hope is rekindled. If this is you, where do you see Him? Be assured He is not somewhere you can get to through the old paths, through the empty pursuits that have kept your heart tethered to the earthly realm. Call to Him for clarity and sound direction and then step forth at His command, knowing that it is not in His nature to fail you.

Today's Prayer

Father, I pray that You would reveal Your Word to me and bring clarity to Your call. Bid me to come to You on the water, where the powers of the natural realm yield in every way to Your Word. I thank You for Your grace, faithfulness, and perfect timing. I yield everything to You this day. In the name of Jesus, amen.

Victory to you, my brothers and sisters in Christ,

Today's Scripture

> The Lord bless thee and keep thee. The Lord make His face shine upon thee and be gracious unto thee. The Lord lift up His countenance upon thee and give thee peace. And they shall put my name upon the children of Israel and I will bless them. (Numbers 6:24–27)

Today's Message: Supreme Blessedness

Have you ever been so blessed that you couldn't help but pour it out to others? The intent of the Lord in Creation was to orchestrate the peace and fulfillment of His love through all living creatures. But this design was broken when sin entered the world. His response to the fall of man was the power of His cross to provide forgiveness, new life, and the restoration of the rule of His love. Everything we have and everything we will gain in this world is temporary, but what we have available to us as we learn to yield to His Spirit will encompass both time and eternity.

> And of His fullness have all we received and grace for grace. (John 1:16)

Our words have a great influence on those around us. They can bring hope, guidance, and encouragement to all that they reach. Sometimes we try in our own understanding to speak in a way that will be meaningful to others, but in so doing, we miss something important. The blessing of the Lord is not the word or work of man.

It is a gift of His grace, a touch of His hand, the breath of His presence, and the favor of His redemption. It all flows out from Him.

In this world, we will face hurts and pressures, but God is with us, and He is always speaking. His spoken grace flowing out of His child brings forth the unction of His Spirit, encapsulated in every word. Nothing can stand in the way when His Spirit pours over us and through us. Each time the sun rises, we can be assured that His provision is waiting with care and understanding to both lift us up and to be the healing balm upon another weary soul.

> Blessed be the Lord, who daily loadeth us with benefits, even the God of our salvation. (Psalm 68:19)

Not only can we find God's blessing in times of joy, but also when we are lonely, sad, or disappointed. We sometimes face things that we would never choose for ourselves, but in retrospect, we see that we were enriched and enlarged because of them. When we make happiness our goal, we set ourselves up for grief because pleasures in the temporal realm do not last. But when we seek the Lord, we have an ongoing source of hope and assurance. It bubbles forth and flows continuously, touching our lives with enough to share.

In your quiet time, ask the Lord to make you receptive to Him, discerning what He wants you to share with someone. He will stir your heart with a timely message for them. He will empower you by His Spirit to deliver it in power and conviction. Have you ever experienced a moment when He put someone in your remembrance to pray for or to contact? Has He put a desire in your heart to bless a specific person, and you don't know why? Follow His inner promptings because there is no greater blessing than this for those in need of His touch.

We have all been called to minister by the Spirit. He is too faithful not to come through for you if you are willing to follow His lead. His words are supreme and final. None of them will come back to Him void. On the last day, they will stand and give a faithful account of all they have accomplished and the one through whom they have accomplished it. This work is highly valued by Him, and He will provide everything you need to bless and be blessed in it.

Today's Prayer

Blessed are You, King of kings and Lord of lords, who brings forth provision and blessedness to every child of Yours who seeks to extend the glory of Your Kingdom. I thank You, Father, that I can be confident and trust in You to be faithful in all that You do through me. In Jesus's name, amen and amen.

Victory to you, my brothers and sisters in Christ,

Today's Scripture

> Every man's work shall be made manifest: for the day shall declare it, because it shall be revealed by fire; and the fire shall try every man's work of what sort it is.
>
> If any man's work abide which he hath built thereupon, he shall receive a reward. (1 Corinthians 3:13–14)

Today's Message: Purity of Ministry

What does it mean to walk in purity of ministry before the Lord? We are all called to serve in the Kingdom because we are all members of Christ, who embodies the purest service to God and man. It is the purity of intent that goes through the process of learning how to move by the leading of the Spirit and that cultivates a vertical focus in everything accomplished.

> With good will doing service, as to the Lord and not to men. (Ephesians 6:7)

We are all part of an awakening and a refinement that is taking place on the earth, but few have yet learned to acknowledge the vital role that each person plays, the responsibility of each, and what is at stake. The Kingdom of the Lord is at hand, and we are called and gifted to minister out of the revelation of His love for us and for His people. Our success in this will arise from pure motives and obedience to His leading. When we look at the state of things, it is tempting to be baffled about how we can even *begin* to serve and build. We can be certain that this work is not a process or a system birthed in the mind of man. Our part must be to cultivate a heart that is impartial and always seeking to help others in the way we are led. His ministry through us will flow as a gentle, calm breeze of anointing unique to our individual gifts and callings. He desires pure motivations and a Spirit-led outreach when He empowers. The fullness of emphasis is to continue what Jesus started, to share His heart, to uplift, and to encourage the body of Christ so we can all come to know and experience Him in new and powerful ways.

True Kingdom ministry is manifested when we can move in an open and unrestrained way by the leading of the Spirit, unhindered by earthly agendas. The work will flow naturally according to the way God has made us, without concern that our needs will be met, and all will fall into place through His direction and provision.

> But seek ye first the Kingdom of God and His righteousness; and all these things shall be added unto you. (Matthew 6:33)

So why is the intent of our heart so pivotal to all that the Lord does through us? It is the true, sincere heart that walks with conviction and faithful stewardship of everything provided as everything *is* provided through those around us. Whether financial, organizational, or administrative, He directs all into the hands of those who will deal faithfully with all resources and abilities necessary to the work. We are not all-knowing, so there is no need to concern ourselves with bringing together every part of the whole. It is not numbers or natural abilities that persevere to the end but truth, openness to the Spirit, and a willingness to walk by His leading.

The ministry of the Spirit will not be ruled by the order and techniques of man. It will be led solely by His own presence and power. God has *already* blessed us with all spiritual blessings in Christ, and as we grow in these blessings, we will relinquish all need to operate according to our own understanding and ability. Everything will be experienced with passion and purpose as we walk before the Lord of hosts in the unveiling of this great work we are privileged to be a part of.

Today's Prayer

Abba Father, I thank You that You have chosen me to experience the pure revelation of Your ministry, given freely to be humbly received with conviction, passion, and the willingness to continue what You have started through prayer and worship until the end of time. In Jesus's name, amen and amen.

Victory to you, my brothers and sisters in Christ,

Today's Scripture

> For we are His workmanship, created in Christ Jesus unto good works, which God hath before ordained that we should walk in them. (Ephesians 2:10)

Today's Message: Priceless Masterpiece

What do you consider to be the greatest masterwork of all Creation? When you reflect upon the beauty of Heaven and Earth, where do you think the greatest glory abides? The majesty of God is revealed in everything He has made, but His greatest praise, His crowning splendor, is shown forth, not in what He has created but in what He has *redeemed.* His greatest masterpiece is *you.* You have been taken from the depths of sin and darkness, redeemed and transformed in Christ, and made to sit among your ransomed brethren in righteousness, forever reigning in the light of His presence. This glory of the manifested heart of God has been formed in all perfection and purity, even while dwelling in fallen vessels. We are the eternal Kingdom of redeemed royalty, saved from hell to reign in Heaven. And you have been made to be His beloved child whom He has passionately restored to Himself in great love, never once disowned or rejected, nor should you ever be made to feel that you are not His. No one can separate from Him what He has sanctified and justified. And your inheritance is but one reflection of His heart, one shining facet in the vast Kingdom of His love.

The workmanship of God itself proclaims the extent of His power.

> I will praise thee for I am fearfully and wonderfully made: marvelous are thy works and that my soul knoweth right well. My substance was not hid from thee when I was made in secret and curiously wrought in the lowest parts of the earth. Thine eyes did see my substance, yet being unperfect; and in thy book all my members were written, which in continuance were fashioned, when as yet there was none of them. (Psalm 139:14–16)

We must reject the lie that our lives came about by chance. We cannot entertain such notions when Scripture declares how intimately and intricately the Creator has woven together the vessel that would serve as the tabernacle of His glory. How much more then ought we to acknowledge Him in our redemption and glorification? We have been called and sealed in Christ Jesus, not based upon our own merits but upon the greatness of His love.

> Moreover whom He did predestinate, them He also called: and whom He called, them He also justified, and whom He justified, them He also glorified. (Romans 8:30)

You may feel as though you are not strong enough or smart enough to serve the Lord or to walk in the things of the Kingdom. Or perhaps you are rejected by others and don't know how you could be of any value to God. But these are the standards of worth held by humanity. You are indeed valuable to Him, and when your brokenness makes way for it, you will be a conduit of His power and love. His priceless masterpiece is you. It is you who bears the name of Messiah and who longs to make yourself available to Him. All grace will be provided to stand in the midst of all difficulty as you relinquish all faith in your own strength. This generation of mighty, chosen warriors of God manifesting through broken vessels has the potential to turn the momentum away from the powers of darkness in these last days, creating beacons of hope in the midst of despair. Your life and calling are not for sale, so never compromise them for anything or anyone. You were bought with a priceless ransom on the cross of Calvary and are called to give up the shadow of death for the glory of His life.

Today's Prayer

Heavenly Father, I am grateful that before You even created me, You loved me. I thank You for making me a treasure in Your Kingdom. My heart is sold out to You alone. All Heaven declares the excellence of Your power and love. This is why my heart is in a place of unending worship and praise. I give all glory to You for such a beautiful work of grace and mercy. In Jesus's name, amen and amen.

Victory to you, my brothers and sisters in Christ,

Today's Scripture

> Finally, my brethren, be strong in the Lord and in the power of His might. Put on the whole armor of God that ye may be able to stand against the wiles of the devil. For we wrestle not against flesh and blood but against principalities, against powers, against the rulers of the darkness of this world, against spiritual wickedness in high places. Wherefore take unto you the whole armor of God that ye may be able to withstand in the evil day and having done all, to stand. (Ephesians 6:10–13)

Today's Message: The Indispensable Weapon

Are you ready to take your stand, knowing that there is no greater weapon at your disposal than the sword of the Spirit? Do you truly believe that what the Lord has spoken is enough and that you can be equipped to triumph? When you move to take your place in the Kingdom amidst the battles manifesting around you, you have entered into an ancient struggle that did not originate in the earthly realm. Sometimes our tendency is to retreat from what is coming against us and to suppress the truth of Scripture instead of pressing into the Lord. Sometimes we think the reason we're facing spiritual attacks is because we're doing something wrong when in reality they are a reaction by our adversary to the obedience we have demonstrated. The day you were born of the Spirit, you entered into a conflict that requires spiritual understanding about how to stand by the means He provides.

The more we grow spiritually, the more we will encounter resistance. When we give in to the assaults on our mind, it can cause us to us lose confidence in God to keep us. This leads to depression, anxiety, and spiritual paralysis. The enemy will not stop until you are defeated and you declare yourself unable and unwilling. But the truth is that you are the apple of God's eye, a soul most precious to Him, rescued from darkness and destined to advance His Kingdom! The liberty of the Spirit is within you already, and the more you grow, the more areas of your heart and soul He will liberate. Evil can have no permanent power over you. Though the battles come in intense waves and storms, they are only temporary because a new day has already dawned and the Kingdom of God is within you.

Humility and truth carry great power. We must learn not to fight in the flesh but to rely on the Lord.

> Dearly beloved, avenge not yourselves, but rather give place unto wrath: for it is written, "Vengeance is mine; I will repay, saith the Lord." (Romans 12:19)

Sometimes when we find ourselves under perpetual attack, fear tries to grip our heart. We try to fight from a place of fleshly strength, not remembering that He is in control. We forget our sword, which is the voice of God speaking to the very struggles we are facing.

The Word of the Lord is the greatest weapon we have. It can permeate our souls and activate in our lives when it is illuminated in our hearts by His Spirit. God alone has the power to speak life into our innermost being. The entire universe was created by His Word. The mighty storms are calmed at the sound of His rebuke. None of us on our own have the power to break strongholds or to bring release from bondage. Only God brings deliverance. Only Living Water can cleanse and sanctify us. We can each gain the understanding needed to know His will, to flourish, and to have victory. It is reserved for the child of God to take part in the most fulfilling existence known to man, to tap into a level of Kingdom life and living that is infinitely beyond anything we could ask or imagine.

Today's Prayer

Our majesty on high, I thank You for Your holy sword, my mighty weapon that speaks to my heart in spirit and in truth and fills me with great confidence and boldness. Yours is the only power I long for and need as I walk this path with You. In Jesus's name, amen and amen.

Victory to you, my brothers and sisters in Christ,

Today's Scripture

> Thine, O Lord is the greatness and the power and the glory and the victory and the majesty: for all that is in the heaven and in the earth is thine; thine is the Kingdom, O Lord and thou art exalted as head above all. Both riches and honour come of thee and thou reignest over all; and in thine hand is power and might; and in thine hand it is to make great and to give strength unto all. Now therefore, our God, we thank thee and praise thy glorious name. (1 Chronicles 29:11–13)

Today's Message: Sovereign King

Have you ever considered the mystery of the sovereignty of God? It may feel unsettling to ponder the vastness of His dominion and knowledge, but when we meditate on these truths, we will always be brought back to the cross. The immensity of His power was at work through His Son in great humility to reconcile us to Himself. Jesus was and is completely God and yet also completely man. This speaks to the supremacy of His love. The sovereign King, in all His power and preeminence, is peace, healing, and redemption to us. His Kingdom flows through both spiritual and natural realms and proclaims wholeness to all who receive Him, a wholeness that transcends even the conflict and darkness that war against it.

If you believe that God is sovereign, how does it influence you? How does it impact the way you think and live? We make choices that have a real effect on our lives and upon the lives of those around us. We also have a role in our own maturity. And we are certainly called to obedience and to walk in that which is eternal. However, in truly recognizing that God is sovereign over us and in trusting *Him* to bring us to maturity, we are declaring that our redemption, in all its manifestations, is as good as done. We have a natural tendency to focus on our own performance and abilities instead of resting on His, especially when we find ourselves beset by warfare and trials. We need not be paralyzed with fear when making decisions and taking action. If we make a wrong choice, all is not lost. He has already taken it into account. His faithfulness walks side by side with us, and He can set us back on the right course, even if different settings are used. It is His sovereignty that is the supreme authority over us, and He brings us into who we were created to be in His time and in His way.

The Lord reigns with total power and authority. He is not bound or limited by anything or anyone in all Creation.

> The Lord of hosts has sworn, saying, "Surely as I have thought, so shall it come to pass and as I have purposed, so shall it stand." (Isaiah 14:24)

The way of His dominion is consistent with His attributes, actions, and decrees, and it overrules all human reasoning and disputes. The directives that arise from His foreknowledge stand from the beginning to the end and forever.

> Remember the former things of old: for I am God and there is none else; I am God and there is none like me. Declaring the end from the beginning and from ancient times the things that are not yet done, saying, "My counsel shall stand and I will do all my pleasure." (Isaiah 46:9–10)

If God did not know in advance what would happen, He would not be God. The divine knowledge views every event in time, every thought, every word, and every deed, everything in its pattern, and everyone on their journey with absolute clarity. We can surely be confident and stand in faith that no matter what is going on around us, God will have His way, and it will be good. Trust that the One who says He loves you will justify and demonstrate that love in all ways, even when your world seems completely out of control. He has it all covered from beginning to end.

Today's Prayer

Abba Father, You sit upon the throne of Your holiness and reign over all Creation. Thank You for allowing me to be a part of all You have made. Your great love transcends and covers everything that I am in You. I revere You with my utmost worship, praise, and honor and offer my whole heart and soul to You. In Jesus's name, amen and amen.

Victory to you, my brothers and sisters in Christ,

Today's Scripture

> Rejoice not against me, O mine enemy. When I fall, I shall arise; when I sit in darkness, the Lord shall be a light unto me. (Micah 7:8)

Today's Message: Rise Again

Have you ever noticed just how much the Lord does to enable your recovery from adversity or failure? Throughout our time in this world, we will have many peaks and valleys. Humbly receiving restoration when we stumble and bouncing back after we are overwhelmed are qualities our Father develops within us over time and through experience. Sometimes we feel like giving up during painful battles, not remembering that the key to resilience is faith in God's goodness. He loves to empower us to endure, to cause us to stand back up, and to encourage us to embrace our identity and begin again.

When we have life-changing events that threaten our ability to move on, God will always be there to provide what we need to start anew. This doesn't mean that we become numb to what has happened. It means He gives us the grace to grow from it and to walk free from lasting harm. At times we are also allowed to see this grace upon others and to learn from it. As they refuse to give up, even when heavily burdened, our hope is renewed.

> We are troubled on every side, yet not distressed; we are perplexed, but not in despair; Persecuted but not forsaken; cast down, but not destroyed; Always bearing about in the body

> the dying of the Lord Jesus that the life also of Jesus might be made manifest in our body. (2 Corinthians 4:8–10)

Some of God's people suffer greatly but continue to follow His path. They have learned through time and experience that He is always faithful to restore.

When struggles intensify, we sometimes assume that we know how things are going to go. When situations seem to be headed in a direction that can only be the wrong one, we tend to think our journey will end in ruin. We think we can predict the final outcome, so instead of exercising faith in the Lord, we give up or take matters into our own hands to salvage what we can.

> Trust in the Lord with all thine heart and lean not unto thine own understanding. In all thy ways acknowledge Him, and He shall direct thy path. (Proverbs 3:5–6)

Whenever disaster seems to loom over us, it is wisdom to trust Him rather than rely on our own faulty perceptions.

Simple faith is enough during times of trouble. The resurrection of Jesus was a solemn demonstration of His ability and willingness to redeem, and it remains a solid assurance to us all. The weight of all temporal afflictions in the fallen realm became subject to Him when He came forth from the grave and bestowed upon us a gift beyond measure. None of us can sustain the storms that come against us without His grace and intervention. None can recover from failure without His tender mercies and redemptive power. When He rose from the dead, the hope that we could rise again was assured.

The world can hurt us, but it will never destroy us because God is for us. His mercy and grace follow us and hold us throughout each trial and stand as an anchor for our souls. He is love, power, and perfect wisdom in all His dealings with His people. To know Him is to be moved to give our very lives to Him, being persuaded of His instant forgiveness, intimate fellowship, and joyful restoration of our souls.

Today's Prayer

Papa God, I thank You that Your power to rise again radiates within me in times of uncertainty and challenge. I acknowledge that I am powerless to wrestle with the storms of this fallen world in my own strength. But I am grateful that You lead me to victory through Your faithfulness and by building my confidence in You. Please saturate me with Your presence when I fail and help me to see it all from Your perspective that I may glorify You. In Jesus's name, amen and amen.

Victory to you, my brothers and sisters in Christ,

Today's Scripture

> Finally, my brethren, be strong in the Lord and in the power of His might. (Ephesians 6:10)

Today's Message: Free to Stand

When you suddenly find yourself facing a wave of conflict, are you able to stand firm and stay focused on the Lord, hearing, trusting, and obeying? We can only keep our hearts fixed on Him in the midst of opposition if we are free from the weights and hooks of the natural realm, those subtle, intangible effects of our earthly life that form the basis for our stumbling. The victory we seek will come when the power of the Spirit flows freely through us, and the hindrances that strengthen the flesh and block our way forward are removed.

We grow in our ability to stand as we gain the freedom to act in the power of *His* might. To walk as He walked, we must be unwavering in our passion to be as He is, but this transformation does not take place by our *effort* to be as He is. It happens as we turn our affection toward Heaven and are conformed to His image through fire and water. He alone knows the proper balance of struggle and release and of tribulation and comfort needed to bring forth the warrior He has birthed into His Kingdom. Everything is prescribed with perfect clarity and total authority. He does not operate in your life as someone who simply reacts to what you do but as someone who *knows* you and who is resolute in His zeal to bring you to your expected end. He asks that you forget your flawed responses to His work for they were the reason for the work and for the redemption that followed. Simply stand in the liberty and triumph afforded you by His grace.

The more we cross the threshold between the failure of the flesh and the victory of the Spirit, the more we will encounter the new creation that we are, formed from eternity, predestined to be forever conformed to the image of Christ. No longer will we feel the need to force ourselves to be something we are not because we now understand the difference between the flesh and the Spirit, between our power and His. That which God has designed in Christ is now manifesting in ever-increasing measure, and as we grow in the grace and newness of His Spirit, we simply *are* who we have been made to be. Although we still struggle and stumble and fail at times, the understanding we have gained through our experiences has provided a foundation of hope that leaves us undaunted in our upward progress.

> And not only so, but we glory in tribulations also: knowing that tribulation worketh patience; And patience, experience; and experience, hope. (Romans 5:3–4)

The Lord always seeks to lead us to release and triumph, despite our best efforts to the contrary. Even when it seems that darkness has had its victory over us, we discover that quite the opposite has happened. Death has instead been taken captive by Him and turned against itself in precise blows to the body of death and the motions of sin that hold us captive. The suffering we endure in His will is nothing less than a display of absolute divine authority. He brings the enemy against the very darkness we have given place to and against the strength of our flesh that empowers us to fail. In this very act, our adversary is forced to drive out his own legal right over us. We will truly know that all authority in Heaven and Earth is His when we experience His sovereignty to establish, strengthen, and settle us in every way.

> And having spoiled principalities and powers, He made a shew of them openly, triumphing over them in it. (Colossians 2:15)

Today's Prayer

My Father in Heaven, I long to stand before You in the power of Your Spirit. I know that this requires deep work within me and that without You, I can do nothing. I pray, Father, that You would accomplish this great work in my heart as I give myself to You in every way I can. In the mighty name of Jesus, amen.

Victory to you, my brothers and sisters in Christ,

Today's Scripture

> Blessed be the Lord my strength, which teacheth my hands to war and my fingers to fight. (Psalm 144:1)

Today's Message: Kingdom Warfare

What do you think is the most important element of your struggle against spiritual darkness? What do you see as the greatest key to unlocking victory? We are surrounded by a world that operates in a way that is completely different from the Kingdom of God, especially with regard to warfare. Yet the Lord has overcome the world and has given His people the grace to overcome it as well. Sometimes the simplest concepts in the Kingdom are the farthest from our reach because they bear the starkest contrast to what we are accustomed to. But the things that are impossible to master on our own are this way because of our need to walk them out in union with our conquering King.

The kingdom and domain of darkness has taught us to fight the way that it fights but the Lord has called us to overcome darkness in the way that *He* fights. This requires a complete reversal of our understanding of how true authority operates, and it calls for our cooperation in learning how to walk and wield His authority properly. He has gone before us and won the victory, but the way that He did so was through death and resurrection. He calls upon His people to overcome in the same way: by making ourselves of no reputation, by taking upon ourselves the form of a servant, and by walking in obedience to the leading and empowerment of the Spirit. These are the actions that removed our adversary from his seat of power and to this day continue to remove his power over the hearts and minds of those held captive by it.

> That I may know Him, and the power of His resurrection, and the fellowship of His sufferings, being made conformable unto His death; If by any means I might attain unto the resurrection of the dead. (Philippians 3:10–11)

We are called to walk with the Lord in the power of His Spirit. But to effectively do this while clothed in earthen vessels, we must recognize our need to have successive elements of our fallen nature broken. It is only then that He can extend His resurrection power through us and pour it into the hearts and lives of His people. His Kingdom advances in this world only through death and resurrection, and His life flows through us in its purest form in the absence of all interference of flesh and mind.

Our union with the Lord is found not only in the kernel of wheat that falls into the ground and dies but also in the abundance of spiritual fruit that springs forth in its place. Through humility and faith in the provision of our Master, we will make our war, and we will stand as more than conquerors in the face of all opposition as will those who have been touched by the life of the Spirit released through us. The flood of darkness that seeks to overthrow us will be eclipsed by the manifold embrace of the Lord of our triumph. Even the joy we find in final victory will be outshined by the glad countenance of our Father, who through all our highs and lows, through all our stumbling and doubts, foresaw this day and rejoices at its arrival. Until then, the overflow of spiritual life pouring through us will bring its transformative power to bear upon each soul who has continued with us in our temptations that together we may be appointed a place at His table forever.

Today's Prayer

My Father, I have witnessed all You have done for me. I have doubted at times that things would happen as You said, but I renew my trust in You, knowing that You only speak the truth. I pray You would take my hand today and walk forward with me through everything I face for I know that in the end, I will be shown that it was all for my good. In the mighty name of Jesus, amen.

Victory to you, my brothers and sisters in Christ,

Today's Scripture

> Let us be glad and rejoice and give honour to Him: for the marriage of the Lamb is come and His wife hath made herself ready. And to her was granted that she should be arrayed in fine linen, clean and white: for the fine linen is the righteousness of saints. (Revelation 19:7–8)

Today's Message: Righteous Dominion

In what ways do you see your relationship with the Lord touching those around you? Have you ever contemplated the effects of our *corporate* union with Him? Have you ever wondered how it will look in the ages to come? Each interaction we have with Him generates a powerful spiritual unity that pulses outward in a multitude of ways, instilling life and virtue into everyone with hearts to receive. When these individual connections with Him reproduce, intertwine, and build up His body, they form a stronghold of righteousness that raises His banner over a crumbling kingdom of darkness.

> For we are members of His body, of His flesh and of His bones. (Ephesians 5:30)

We have been joined together in a seamless union with the Lord, being born of His Spirit and drawing our life force from the very heart of who He is. When we serve His people by the anointing, imparting to them the hidden manna of His Person, we provide an avenue for Him to stand before His beloved and to be everything they need Him to be in that moment. When we share in the fellowship of His sufferings, we ascend to the very summit of His passion and purity, embodying the highest expressions of His love and releasing a spiritual power that is stronger than death. With each dying, we rise again to soar higher in the life of His Spirit, bringing a fresh impartation of power and glory to break up the fallow ground in the hearts of His people. If we overcome as He overcame, we will reign with Him as He reigns, expressing in every way that we are bone of His bone and flesh of His flesh.

The righteousness of God imputed to His children can only have as its consummate victory the righteous dominion of the Bride of Christ seated in glory with Him. She will make herself ready through a steadfast commitment to unite with His will in a steady outworking of His nature and grace. Through the mutual edification and empowerment of His people, the defenses will be strengthened, and the city will stand, even in the midst of gross darkness. To her, it will be granted to be arrayed in living garments reflecting every facet of grace and beauty that flows from the heart of her Bridegroom.

Today the city of God spans the earth in scattered pockets of light, each bearing witness to a unique portion of the authority and majesty of the King. Each individual and corporate witness is refined by grace, bearing dim reflections of the Lord through veils of flesh. One day, each reflection will be magnified to perfection, each turning of the heart to Him in love and obscurity will be acknowledged and rewarded, and the dispersed light of the Bride will be raised from the dust of the earth and brought together to reign with Him forever. Allow this hope to burn in your heart. We are waiting for the Lord to return, but He is also waiting for *us*, patiently bringing us forth and preparing our works before us that we may be clothed forever in everything He has made us to be.

> Beloved, now are we the sons of God and it doth not yet appear what we shall be: but we know that when He shall appear we shall be like Him; for we shall see Him as He is. (1 John 3:2)

Today's Prayer

Dear heavenly Father, I am thankful that You have granted me this relationship with You. I know that what You are accomplishing in me is far more than I dare imagine, but I have tasted of it, and I am persuaded of its realness. Please take me deeper and help me to share this experience with those You have called to my side that we all may love and enjoy You forever. In the precious name of Jesus, amen.

Victory to you, my brothers and sisters in Christ,

Today's Scripture

> To him that overcometh will I grant to sit with me in my throne, even as I also overcame and am set down with my Father in His throne. (Revelation 3:21)

Today's Message: The Throne of Victory

What do you consider to be the deepest expression of the Father's joy over His children? To answer this question, we need to look no further than the image of God reflected in an earthly father's devotion to his child.

> If ye then, being evil, know how to give good gifts unto your children, how much more shall your Father which is in Heaven give good things to them that ask Him? (Matthew 7:11)

Your trajectory in the Spirit has been ordained by the Lord to bring you into the highest possible inheritance in His Kingdom. He has already taken all things in your life into account from the beginning to the end and has mingled your every success and failure with His perfect wisdom and absolute goodness.

We cannot say that we were born of the Spirit, having been raised from the dead, having had our sins blotted out, having been partakers of the victory of His cross, without also acknowledging that He is the God of abundant triumph. Have you truly tasted and seen that He is rich unto all who call upon Him? He has beautified our death with His resurrection. He has taken the wages of our sin and offered us a death conformable to His own, thereby rewarding us. Will He not also bring forth good from every lesser scheme against our soul? It is the spiritual poverty of our religion that has narrowed our view of God. We have limited Him, but He has not consented to our limitations. He has overrun our feeble protests against His goodness with promises to do far more for us than we could ever conceive.

> Now unto Him that is able to do exceeding abundantly above all that we ask or think, according to the power that worketh in us, unto Him be glory in the church by Christ Jesus throughout all ages, world without end. Amen. (Ephesians 3:20–21)

The nature of our relationship with the Lord extends far beyond union because it is far more than a union. It is *transformation* freely granted, and it makes us partakers of both His nature and His inheritance.

> He that overcometh shall inherit all things, and I will be his God and he shall be my son. (Revelation 21:7)

We are now the body of Christ, and He cannot deny us the highest possible portion in His Kingdom because He cannot deny Himself. It is indeed up to us to apprehend that which we have been apprehended for in Christ, but even the least in the Kingdom is far greater than the greatest on Earth because the victory of His resurrection resides within us. We stand as He stands: victorious over death, reigning in life, and inheritors of a Kingdom that will never fade away.

Embrace the Lord's victory, for it has already embraced you. You cannot die, except to put off the body of death. If you suffer because you have chosen His will and His ways, own the truth that your suffering is not worthy to be compared with the glory and consolation that will arise because of it. We need only wait a little while longer, and everything written will be manifested on a deeply personal level. The earth will be bathed in His glory, and His people will be baptized in His triumph as all tears are wiped away, and His beloved children delight themselves in His goodness, in each other, and in the abundance of His glorious rest.

Today's Prayer

God of immeasurable grace and blessing, I stand in awe of You. Everything You have done for me is magnificent and final. I thank You, Lord Jesus, that Your throne is my throne, that Your victory is my victory, and that everything You are and do is my eternal lot. I wait in love and joy for You to return that Your every promise to Your people may become our reality. In the wonderful name of Jesus, amen.

ABOUT THE AUTHORS

Michael and Julie Battaglini currently live in Rochester, Minnesota, with their dog Mordechai. They were married in 2014, and the Father has mingled their unique combination of gifts and callings to produce a deep and rich ministry of His Spirit through them. They are involved in a home-church fellowship and have a passion to see the Kingdom of God flourish in the hearts and lives of those around them.

Each day, Julie ministers to and prays for the sick and hurting. The Lord uses her to bring healing and refreshing to those He brings across her path, some of whom have come seeking medical care in Rochester as their last hope. She receives numerous testimonies from people who tell her of the spiritual, physical, and emotional healing they have received from Him during their time in Rochester. It was in this context that she felt led to begin writing letters of hope and encouragement to those whom she had prayed for and handing them out wherever the Lord directed her.

Michael and Julie's ministry of the written word has become a demonstration of the simplicity that God so often chooses to work through. He has continued to expand the depth and power of His anointing through them as they simply make themselves available to extend the reach of His love and kindness to His children. It has been their strong desire to model this informal approach to imparting the life and power of the Spirit that others may know that they too can discover their place in God's Kingdom.